LADY, YOU SHOT ME

A COLLECTION OF POEMS
by Darren C. Demaree

8th House Publishing
Montreal, Canada

Copyright © 8th House Publishing 2018
First Edition

Published worldwide by 8th House Publishing.
Front Cover Design by 8th House Publishing

ISBN 978-1-926716-52-7

Designed by 8th House Publishing.
www.8thHousePublishing.com

Set in Adobe Garamond Pro, Bitter, LD Music and Raleway.

LIBRARY AND ARCHIVES CANADA CATALOGUING IN PUBLICATION

Demaree, Darren C., author
    Lady, you shot me : a collection of poems / by Darren C. Demaree.

ISBN 978-1-926716-52-7 (softcover)

    1. Cooke, Sam--Poetry. I. Title.

PS3604.E56L33 2018   811'.6   C2018-906497-8

Thanks

Many thanks to authors Peter Guralnick and Daniel Wolff, as their respective biographies were instrumental in supplementing and expanding my knowledge and understanding of Sam Cooke. Many thanks to the Whetstone Branch of the Columbus Library for giving me a wide birth while I read and took many notes on the music and narratives of Sam Cooke. Finally, thank you to my wife and children for allowing me the time to go all the way down the rabbit hole with this project. It began as hero-worship, and evolved very quickly into a much more complex study on the damage a famous man was able to inflict on the women in his life. That evolution took time, and my family gave me the time I needed to process everything through these poems.

— *Darren C. Demaree*

CONTENTS

Dedication

For John Oswalt, an all-time friend, who started this research with me long ago when we were trying to write a screenplay about the recording of the "Live at the Harlem Club" album.

Lady, You Shot Me
Darren C. Demaree

JANUARY 22, 1931

Even the Mississippi Delta
possesses a caped heart
& everything that is used to

flooding, floods in joy
& deconstructs in joy
as well. Some floods, though,

simply wash the legs
of a child clean
& that is the opposite

of a shipwreck.
That constant
ebb spreads to cape

another heart,
spreads to protect joy,
to let the man find song.

A SWEET MISSISSIPPI ACCENT

Some smoothness
is simple enough
to be an actual wolf.

LADY, YOU SHOT ME #1

Deep in the aggregate
of the utmost of the extreme
of each person whose hands

touched to break through
the ground, but broke through
each other terribly. No one

was saved. They were all
victims. The body bag took
only the darkest-skinned

of the bodies. Even the fat
roses refused to bloom
for a while after all of that.

DECORATING THE PHRASE

Every word
shares two skins
with the tongue

that releases it
into the world
& Sam Cooke

could lift
& separate
the same word

fifteen times
in a row
& you would

still believe
there was a soul
in the repetition.

CROP

Some shouting
leaves the song
before the stalk

has been granted
any weight at all
& that loop washes

nothing in the dirt
& rises, rises
with freedom.

Some songs
begin with a tether,
but they never end

that way
& if they try to
they become hymn

for a God
that might allow
such harness

to be attached
to the rockets
of one man

opening
the back of his throat
to charge the heavens.

LADY, YOU SHOT ME #4

The air was all edges
that night
& every collision

left ribbons of human
flesh flapping
like a new tongue

trying to explain why
the breath was vanish-
ing. The whiskey

was left in the car.
The women, in panic,
tasted the cuts

from the jewels
& found that
blood has no song.

AN EASTER CONCERT

Following Jesus
& R.H. Harris
& those well-tailored

hustlers of God
that always had
their Cadillac's in idle

in case the congregation
found out what
there was to find out

was difficult for Sam Cooke,
but if any man could
make mercy sound good

it was him. It took Jesus
thirty-three years to
bring the house down.

Sam was the closing
act from the age
of only nineteen

& when he was found
dead, barely dressed,
surrounded by crying women

& robbed of his money
& his ecstatic calls as well,
the churches went silent

one more time, just in case
it was possible for him
to find the spirit again.

NINETY DAYS ON A MORALS CHARGE

Caught up
in sharing a fuck story
with his girlfriend,
Sam left the lone
page of pornography
alone in her house

& when her little sister
brought the funny thing
to her classroom
the next day it led
back to him. He did
ninety days

in the shallow end
of loss. He watched
that end deepen.
He never talked about
the meaning or risk
in the meaning

of his time in jail,
but he knew
that any time the cops
but their hands on you,
they might finish the job
before you ever learned

a lesson. Frightened into
anchoring a rhythm, he spun
only for show once he got
clear of those walls. He kept
most of the fuck stories
to himself after that.

THERE WERE SEVEN LETTERS IN "SAM COOK"

A name with an odd count
keeps one finger
in the bad black, the dark

that refuses to sparkle at night
& if you can swallow
that level of insecurity

then you can change your name
slightly as an emergence
into the mythic.

I can't think of a man they made
a statue out of whose name
was only seven letters long.

We have lost almost all
of those seven-letter men
to the simple scars

of simple lives
& since we never heard them
sing, it doesn't matter.

LADY, YOU SHOT ME #5

The clay must harden
to chip bits of it off. Damp,
she used the tips

of hot lead to solidify
& pierce the man, statue(d)
him quickly, took the first

wrinkles in his face
& cemented them there
forever. That was terrible

art. That was inevitable.
She had the gun behind
the counter for a reason.

SISTER FLUTE

Dressed better than an angel
& moving like hands that never touch
furniture, some women

are more important than the chapel
& those women can become the chapel
if they can shake loose the carcass

of Jesus fast enough. Those shards
of faith can glisten, can look alive
if you have a Sister Flute dancing.

"THE GORGEOUS SAM COOKE"
- *Darlene Love, singer and actress*

The light can cluster
& collect the hotlings
& lead any god out

of the room. That is
how he took over
all of those small chapels

& those daughters
of the traveling preachers.
He was gorgeous

& without shame.
There was guilt, sure,
but no one can see that

when you move
like a flare in the darkness
of a youth's first arousal.

"LORD, HE SPENT SO MUCH TIME IN FRONT OF THAT MIRROR"

-   *Gloria Jones, member of The Blossoms*

Part of the vision
persists. The small
separation of gums

& that naked device
of a smile would
turn a reflection

into a movie screen.
Of course he stared
at himself, everyone

else already was
& that mad taste
of self, affirmed

incredibly, constantly
offered up the idea
that if he didn't look

at himself as well,
he might be missing
something important.

LADY, YOU SHOT ME #7

He wanted to give away
his heart

& the police
in Los Angeles

wanted to catalog his heart.
They did the least

they could.
The absolute least.

SEDUCING ARETHA FRANKLIN

He had the other Soul
Stirrers watching the door
in case Reverend Franklin

found out which room he
& Aretha were in, sitting
on the bed, negotiating

her young landscape
& those brothers did their job
when Rev found the right room

they moved him on, despite his anger,
but to hear that voice, that tone
so close to her shot at intimacy

with Sam must have been
just enough brakes to calm
the loving sequence. He could

have been quick with her,
but nobody, nobody thought
you should rush a girl

that could do the things
she could do. She was all
syrup. She left sugar behind.

CITIFIED MUSIC

The sigh is a beat
in the dip
of the girl

who just got off work
& if her hair drags
into the blossom

you must swing her
even faster,
until the blur

takes the buildings
& makes them citizens
that dip as well,

like the music
can move the mountains
of active men

consumed,
but not consumed
by real smoke.

CROSSING OVER

Between the world
of the church
& the wilderness

is a whole collection
of white folks
with money to burn.

LADY, YOU SHOT ME #14

The air, thick
with gun smoke
from three bullets

fired into
the violent, spoken
words of a man,

hung the man,
hung the words
as a ghost

that found
no cloth to soak
or light to catch

& yet, he said
these words to touch
the disturbance.

A HARMONY SO TIGHT YOU
COULD SEE IT IN THE AIR

If you can see between
the water
& the remaining

dusts of the waterway,
then you can color
the walking

of the melody
as it sashays into
your heart. We might

be *in a sad mood*,
but that crisp melancholy
gives us hope, even

in a pronounced silence.
I've seen good men
& women do gymnastics

at the idea of music.
If there is a music to save
us, we must rub it

all over our bodies,
until the scent overwhelms
the rest of the empty air.

THE NOTE-BENDER

That absolute height
was unobtainable,
so Sam used a bend,

a curlicue, a back arch
& a misrule of a smile
to take the crowd with him

past his fastened range.
He didn't salvage
a failing, he mouthed it

& played with it, producing
it like a cherry stem tied
into a bow, for everybody

to marvel at. He never
could hit that high note,
but he never needed to.

He was Sam Cooke
& since there was a crowd
he was without weakness.

ATTRACTIVE ENOUGH TO GET AWAY
WITH PRACTICALLY ANYTHING

All pivot
& no drag,

there is no need
to scrimmage

if you're beauty
& beauty

without a shard
of the past.

If you're young
enough to carry

smile only,
no reputation

& the spine
of America

has yet to flex
with your weight

you can damn near
fuck the whole town

& the town after
the town after

that as well. It ends
ugly, of course,

but the beginning
must feel blessed.

LADY, YOU SHOT ME #16

Don't fight it,
the feeling always
burns at first.

Don't fight it,
the feeling always
confuses the witness.

Don't fight it,
the feeling always
ends with a shutter.

Don't fight it,
the feeling is always
a story we tell.

SAYING "I LOVE YOU" FIFTEEN TIMES IN A ROW

There is no peace
in the fattening up
of one's emotional

declarations. Those
words can become
the weight only

& possessing no bones
smother to smother
to smother the ears

in a desire the heart
can never register.
Love becomes dark matter

if it appears to have
no beginning
& no hope of ending.

"SAM MADE THIS SCHOOL GIRL PREGNANT AND NEVER CAME FOR THIS LETTER"
- from a note filed away at Specialty Records

Sam knew the girl was pregnant,
that she had moved to D.C.
to have the baby and give away
the baby, so she could go back
to high school. There was no need
for the extra judgment from
the mail clerk at Specialty Records
to attach that note. Sam knew
that child didn't really count.
He knew that the girl still loved
watching him on television
& that she wouldn't be trouble.
She was giving up the child anyway
& he would never have to grant
that little body more than the spare
spark of life almost already
consumed by the absence
of the memory of actual love.

LADY, YOU SHOT ME #17

His inner version
of the story
is all whiskey

& roaring
& the fires
that tried to burn

inside his body
like they could with-
out consuming him.

It was arson
that killed Sam Cooke;
those bullets

were only the last
logs to be tossed
onto his final flame.

AND THE KIDS WERE GOING TO RIOT

Red ecstatic
& spun together,

of course the police
wanted to shut down

the show
if the kids

were becoming
the show

& since, the police
were all white

they felt like they
might be drowning

in a black sea
which held a rhythm

they could never
match

with their moon-
faces turned up

in confusion.
It was Louisville

& they relented,
because they had

no idea what was
actually happening.

SOMEBODY CUT JESSE BELVIN'S TIRES

The white band
never showed up
& Jessie

& Jackie Wilson
& Little Willie John
& Arthur Prysock

didn't want the second
crowd, the white kids
to miss out

on a Friday night
dance, but they
were pissed about it

& when they got
shouted down
& had the pistols pointed

at their heads
they sped out of town
without checking

if anybody had fucked with
their cars. Somebody
cut Jessie Belvin's tires

& he lost control
on the highway
& he died

& his wife died
& the other driver died
& nobody remembers why

because later that week
somebody bombed
the house of a student

that had integrated,
but Wilson
& Prysock, who both

had their tires slashed
as well remembered.
They passed Hope,

Arkansas
& they pulled over,
short of their own demise,

but so far from safety
that they couldn't sit down
in the gas station.

THAT NIGHT IN GEORGIA

The busses at the airport
couldn't fit one more black man
& colored taxis cab drivers weren't allowed

to come to the airport
without the fear of losing their license
& there, Sam Cooke sat, miles

& years away from the crowd
that was waiting for him,
the city that had already unpacked

to be packed again in the club
& there was the man they wanted
most to hear sing, muttering to himself,

swearing to himself, using
all of the words he could never say
out loud in the South

& that is how the story ended,
without music, without hero,
with only an anxious turning of time.

LADY, YOU SHOT ME #18

He was a figure
out of the metal
of race, bent to

be broken by races
other than his own
& with that abyss

filled by success,
he walked over
mountains of blades

held my white men.
It's fitting that he
survived all of that

& was killed by
a black woman. That,
we knew was coming.

He never guarded
himself from the imp-
ending entry points.

WHEN CASSIUS CLAY ONLY WANTED TO TALK ABOUT SAM COOKE

It matters
most
who says

your name
with reverence
& if the ring

gives us one
champion
who gives us

one champion,
then that,
more than any

other
is the name
we need

to be calling
with the taste
of adrenaline

clinging
to each
syllable.

AFTER THE STEERING WHEEL PLUNGED THROUGH EDDIE CUNNINGHAM'S STOMACH

So near where Bessie Smith died
because of an accident on Highway 61
& because nobody
would treat a black woman
in West Memphis,
Eddie Cunningham died as well
in the middle of surgery,
which we can call progress
I suppose
& Sam Cooke needed to be shuttled
to a different hospital,
a safer hospital,
because there hadn't actually been
much progress in most of Memphis.
Lou Rawls got good treatment
because he was a veteran.
Sam made it out without much
damage done.
Eddie, according
to all of them, said "Shit. God
dammit. Shit. God dammit,"
for the rest of their days.
That refrain never got in the way
of the music,
but these were men
as well, accustomed to the burials,
accustomed to the haunting,
but never used to the visuals of hate
that would always blindside them.

LADY, YOU SHOT ME #20

You will always want
the dark subject
brought into the light,

but if you're asking me
for all of the answers
to a black man's death

in 1964, when only
the shooter, the hooker
& the L.A.P.D. know

what might have gone
down, then you're
asking too much of me.

TEN GRAND

There was a price
to get each woman
to stay out of court

to stay out of the papers,
to stay five hundred feet
away from Sam Cooke

& that price of doing
business was factored in
& deducted with each

new set of papers
from the judge. Sam
had the money

& ten grand, that was
enough to buy
some silence from

their seething.
As long as Bumps
wrote those checks

& intercepted that mail,
the man could sing
& believe

he was Sam Cooke
& that is was enough
truth for his smile.

HIS FIRST "REAL" CHILD

The practice children
were important

to learn what
almost love might be

& since you can
never hear a child

screaming
from any real distance,

they must have been
a joy to forget,

an abstract worship
too vague

to be anything other
than a self-con-

firmation of sorts,
they breathed

in spite of your breath.

LADY, YOU SHOT ME #22

If you put your hands on a woman
& she runs away from you, you
better believe the next woman

you put your hands on without
her permission is going to shoot
you three times in the chest.

If the blood splatter reaches back
to her body, then you were
too god damn close to her trigger.

DELORES DIED HORRIBLY

Imagine you could fit a star,
a burning fireball, a shot heaven
in your mouth

& then the fire moved on
into the world. The scars
in your mouth would never stop

bleeding. You would never be
healed. You were safer
without the star rotating, digging

into your cheeks, but since
that was the only world you knew
for a while, you would miss the pain

& when the pain is what you miss,
you tend to do anything to feel
terrible again. Dee, she

couldn't seduce Nat King Cole,
so she waited for Sam to return
& leave again

& when that happened
one more time, she got real drunk
& drove her car into a building.

It was no accident that she split
her head completely open
& that got Sam to be gentle

as he sparked amidst her grave.

FOR THE GOOD LIFE

It was one of the two things
they did well together, Sam
& Barbara, they split,
never shared all of that money
& if you're busy handling
all of that money, you never have
to handle anything else
& since Sam always preferred
to have his hands around
another women, she got even
more money for her trouble.

ON THE SAME DAY MEDGAR EVERS WAS LAID TO REST

The tangled crowd in Arlington
cried out loud, cried beyond the cemetery
& at the same time, on the same day,
Sam Cooke was left to straighten the tie
of his dead boy, his eighteen-month old
son who found the pool too deep,
too uncontrolled to exist without his
memory in it forever. That ended Sam,
the version of Sam that always had fun,
always took the drink, the girl, the drink
& when he blamed Barbara
for not seeing the boy find the pool,
for being too hungover to chase the toddler
away from danger, his sorrow
took the night, took all of the nights
until his last night took him with it.

GOD AND SAM COOKE'S DEAD SON

Some chainlink,
the view of chainlink

allows as much glory
as possible, but that

same chainlink,
the deluge of chainlink

does nothing to stop
the water forced

through the chainlink
& that beyond

the chainlink
is the same drowning

in the same yard
of chainlink

that swallows our boys
amidst the shape

of a world that drowns
us all in the chainlink

we sometimes mishear
as the music of on high.

LADY, YOU SHOT ME #36

If I had a hammer,
I would have busted up
Sam Cooke's cherry

red Ferrari, kept him
at home that night. Let
him order a woman

over the phone, instead
of chasing down a girl
while wearing four robes

of whiskey. If I had a hammer,
I would make injured citizens
out of each of his ankles

& gone to jail (Do they jail
white men in Los Angeles?)
to get one more live show.

JIM BENCI

Curiouser
& cursiouser

the turning
language

of a man
that procures

women
for friends,

allows his hinge
to slide

with gang
mentality

& never, ever
allows

the girls
their own name,

only the names
of the men

they've been with
& this,

exactly this
is the problem.

"CAT'S DICK GETS HARD, HE'S LIABLE TO DO A WHOLE LOT OF WEIRD THINGS"
-     *Cliff White*

After all thirteen moons
of a rush races past the mind
& the eel raises above the sand
to exist in contact with nothing
but the man's desire, then
all bets are off? This isn't
mythology. It's biology
& an explanation for the blood
that pushes into the penis
& frees the man from his plan
of humanity? This isn't mythology.
It's a terrible history of excuses
& not one of them explains
away why Sam Cooke died
just past his Jesus year.

LADY, YOU SHOT ME #38

I know one
from two

& there were
three people,

at least,
responsible

for Sam Cooke
drowning

in his own blood
& that means

the field is still
at risk,

because, never,
never, never

have we confirmed
how many

victims there were
that night.

I DON'T BELIEVE SAM COOKE TRIED TO RAPE LISA BOYER

It's true, drunk men hear only the voices
in their own head,
but this man was all show

& weakness, the moment a flash of anger
or fear would have passed in front of him,
he would have folded

inside the rest of that whiskey
& called it a night. He was never a good man,
but he was dynamic enough to know

he didn't need to use explosives
to take down the walls of a woman.
I grant you, that monsters are born

in the spur of the moment, but leaving
every practiced cue behind in one night
of active drinking seems like less

of a process than would be required
to translate Sam into an actual beast.

LADY, YOU SHOT ME #43

Sugar dumpling,
sparkling stem
of his sore tissues,

your high-blue softens
while his matter
becomes soundless.

FOR SENTIMENTAL REASONS

I do not believe
Sam Cooke was shot
to death

because he was terrible
to women. I believe
he was shot to death

because he broke down
a door. That shit
will scare anybody.

THE FRAME QUICKLY RIPPED LOOSE

How beautiful
& terrifying
the accepted son

must have looked
barreling through
the motel office door

& with the force
of his only pronoun
lost in the residual

gunfire, his difficulty
was, as it had always
been, how easy

he moved from room
to room, without
thinking about

what it could mean
if he wasn't invited,
nor desired at all.

The inverse of a cape,
they must have thought
for a while

about carrying him
out on the slab
that door became.

LADY, YOU SHOT ME #44

Disrobed,
Sam Cooke
was ready

for action
& when he
was ready,

there was
always
some action

to be had.
The mistake
he made

was forcing
the gun
to be pulled.

Sam Cooke
didn't believe
in safe words

& that is why
we lost him
to the chaos.

BERTHA FRANKLIN

Run over
& run over,
she was

a whole
gallery
of red

deepening
into a pool.
She was old

enough to be
terrified
by the naked

Sam Cooke
& when she
shot the naked

Sam Cooke,
she did so
three times.

The snail always
sharpens over
a rough time.

LADY, YOU SHOT ME #46

There was one person
incredibly relieved
that Sam Cooke

was planted
in the terrible carpet
of that office

& she was still shaking
& she was still staring
at the door

he had broken through
& she was still sure
he would get back up

again, like right after
she had shot him
& he kept coming

for her neck. She thought
she might have shot
a criminal. She might

have been right, but that
is a difficult thing
for me to understand.

HE WAS WEARING AN OVERCOAT, ONE SHOE, AND NOTHING ELSE

Love was the wrong word,
but even the bullets wanted
their way with Sam Cooke.

LADY, YOU SHOT ME #52

Beyond the motel fence,
the fifteen hundred dollars
is still missing from Sam's

coat. What if he was seduced,
robbed, shot to cover it up?
Where is that fifteen hundred

dollars? You don't break down
a door, or assault a woman
over fifteen hundred dollars

if you're Sam Cooke, but what
if he wasn't an asshole, if he
just walked out of that bathroom

too soon to be robbed
peaceably? It's tough to take
a loss if you're almost all whiskey

& untended erection,
but I want to find enough room
to not bury him with the blame.

THE BRAND NEW CHERRY-RED FERRARI

The remainder
is loss; sugar still
in the shape

of a cube
& when Cooke's
body never made it

back into his car,
we knew exactly how
much sweetness

would be tossed
away. How sad
& indelicate

it must have been
for that car to leave
the motel lot

& go through
so many green lights
with no star

behind the wheel.

LADY, YOU SHOT ME #57

If she had taken off
her panties
& then taken off

would you, Sam, have
blown up the building?
She left you. She

took some money
& left you
with your own erection

& you broke down doors?
If you had seen her
drip to drip

& not for you at all,
would you have killed
that woman

in the office
before she killed you?

"NONE SEEMS TO BELIEVE THE STORY BEHIND THE KILLING"

- a funeral director to a local L.A. paper

Sure, she was young
& he was damn drunk
& rich enough to show
the whole world
he was rich enough to be
damn drunk, to be taken

while he was drunk
& when the girl
disappeared into the night
he was drunk enough
to feel taken. What if,
what if, what if he was

taken? Robbed? Tricked
by a girl who wanted Sam
Cooke to give up a little
Sam Cooke? I believe
the girl when she says
she ran scared

& though a polygraph
given by the white cops
of Los Angeles
about a dead black man
is a fictitious thing,
she passed it clean.

What if, what if, what if
that bottle of whiskey
rolling around his cherry-
red Ferrari was most guilty
for the entire scene crashing
instead of unfolding?

"I DON'T LIKE THE WAY HE WAS SHOT. I DON'T LIKE THE WAY IT WAS INVESTIGATED."

-    *Muhammed Ali*

The world was already wild
& when there was almost no
cross-examination of the witnesses

& when the police took the body
to the morgue like nobody would
claim Sam Cooke, the questions

were left to flap against the raw skin
of the black community
& Ali knew, that if his friend

had been a Beatle, the fucking FBI
would have been all over this
& those guys weren't citizens

of this country. The only reality
everyone was left with was a reality
that pushed their love into the ground

without even a long look at justice
or at least a version of justice
that finally explained what happened.

LADY, YOU SHOT ME #61

Shoulders are
as good as mist

if the rest of the man
is only pudding

for the floor to taste,
a final judgment.

WHEN BOBBY WOMACK WORE SAM COOKE'S CLOTHES TO SAM COOKE'S FUNERAL

"Dig that shit," rose above
the din of the crowd

while Womack walked
a little too close to the Cooke

family, swimming in
the dead man's wardrobe,

drowning in the quick hiss
of everyone that recognized

the elaboration of bad timing
& since the sore spot

refused to leave the funeral
everyone waited for the prelude

to begin so they could mourn
without watching

that petty fucker drape
his arms around the remnants

of an authentic idol.
By the time Lou Rawls

began to sing, they had
already talked about burying

Bobby beneath Sam's coffin.
They should have done it.

DEFINITE SADNESS

After the crowd wept,
broke down, screamed
& kicked the pews

& Bessie Griffen collapsed
before she could sing a note
of the last goodbye to Sam,

Brother Ray Charles
put his hand on the casket
& without preparation

got into "Angels Watching
Over Me" to make sure
that most of the business

for the foreseeable future
would be that of grieving
& nothing other than that.

IN 1965, BOBBY WOMACK WAS AN ASSHOLE, BUT IT WASN'T REALLY HIS FAULT

To be twenty
& in love with the wrong woman,
a widowed woman

who dresses you up
in her dead husband's clothes
& makes you sing his songs

& collides with your body
like an atom that must be split
to save the whole world

she's constructed
for the two of you to play in,
that is a motion

that makes a young man
tuck his arms behind his back
& allow whatever may come.

Barbara made him a faithful
version of Sam Cooke
& that must have been pleasant

for her. Still, Bobby,
when you told the press
that his kids were calling

you "Daddy",
dammit man, you should
have known better.

THE POLICE CAUGHT LISA BOYER

Only a month after
the second baptism,
the blood baptism

of Sam Cooke,
the police caught the girl
who wasn't a prostitute

the police had said,
being a prostitute
they now said

& that the fifty dollars
they had entrapped her
with seemed like proof

that she hadn't taken
fifteen hundred dollars
from his wallet

on the night of his death,
but that was a conclusion
they weren't eligible

to make anymore.
She was arrested this time,
without headline.

DREAM BOOGIE, NIGHTMARE BOOGIE
- for Peter Guralnick

Pure velocity, the war
of a man being a man
& the shape of the hole

he leaves in a wall
when he's busy escaping
the room he's been given

& that is only the story
of the man. How he moves
after that, matters more

because of how often
he will dervish into bodies
that don't belong to him.

LADY, YOU SHOT ME #62

Seasick
from the motion
of blame,

I now run
dead-silent through
the gory scene

to place my lips
on Sam Cooke's lips
& I tell him

that he wasn't
a monster,
that he was almost

something tremendous
& terrifying
& almost

gets a lot
of black men killed
in this country.

I was almost
a monster, as well,
for most of my youth

& I survived
mostly because
I was white.

That part
of his death
haunts me still.

WHEN MEN TALK ABOUT SAM COOKE

The slant is freezing
& the silence that follows
after the songs stop

playing, after we hear
just how prideful he was
& important during

the movement's first progress
of the sixties, what comes
next is always nothing;

they've fleshed him out
just enough to be shot
with great mystery.

Nickel to a dollar, those
men will name the women
Sam Cooke mounted

as a flap of character,
as an ornery way to clap
him on the back

for being Sam Cooke
& I, to join the chorus
first made a list of the women

he ruined during the process,
how they struggled, how
they died to leave

those children behind
with their own parents.
He tortured these women

with short visits
& tremendous promises
& that voice they could always

hear on the radio, so powerful,
so soothing, but two and a half
minutes was all he was good for.

RUBBING THE BREATH

The universe
out of nothing,

a song out of
the will

& fear that
the universe

might not be
more than silence.

Acknowledgements

Some of these poems have appeared previously in publications the author and publisher would like to acknowledge.

Alexandria Quarterly: "A Sweet Mississippi Accent", "Citified Music", & "Sister Flute"

Bitchin' Kitsch: "On The Same Day Medgar Evers Was Laid to Rest"

Convergence : "An Easter Concert"

Damfino: "There Were Seven Letters in Sam Cook"

Empty Sink: "For Sentimental Reasons"

Eunoia: "Lady, You Shot Me #7"

Inkwood Indiana: "Lady, You Shot Me #14"

Red Rock: "Lady, You Shot Me #1"

Saubade: "None Seems to Believe the Story Behind the Killing"

Wax Paper: "January 22, 1931"

Welter: "The Gorgeous Sam Cooke"

Ygdrasil: "Seducing Aretha Franklin" & "When Men Talk About Sam Cooke"

ABOUT THE AUTHOR

DARREN C. DEMAREE is the recipient of a 2018 *Ohio Arts Council Individual Excellence Award*, the *Louise Bogan Award* from *Trio House Press*, and the *Nancy Dew Taylor Award* from *Emrys Journal*. He is the Managing Editor of the Best of the Net Anthology and Ovenbird Poetry. He is currently living in Columbus, Ohio with his wife and children. "Lady, You Shot Me" is his tenth collection of poetry.

A SELECTION OF OTHER POETRY TITLES
BY 8TH HOUSE PUBLISHING

MANY FULL HANDS APPLAUDING INELEGANTLY by Darren C. Demaree
5.25 x 8.5 | 194 pages | ISBN 978-1-926716-41-1 (pbk.) | $19.88

Darren C. Demaree's *Many Full Hands Applauding Inelegantly* is as masterful as it is subtle. In this latest collection, Demaree continues to expand and develop not only his power and voice, but the voice of a time and a generation. A transcendent unity runs through this tripartite collection of poems that can be taken individually, as particles or a moment on a continuous wave. Birth (A Violent Sound in Almost Every Place), Life (We are Arrows) and Death (All the Birds Are Leaving) are woven together on the circle that surrounds and unites all.

MAVOR's BONES by Rolli (Charles Anderson)
5 x 8 | 121 pages. ISBN 978-1-926716-30-5 (pbk.) | $15.88

Charles Anderson (Rolli) does it again. In another clever, witty and touching collection, Rolli rollicks again through gardens and cemeteries peopled with dreams, goddesses, characters dead and alive, dukes stricken within gout, gracious skeletons and morose angels.

"I have been dreaming / those dreams of meaning / that come from the waters / of dreaming deep / like drowned men / to the gold skin / of the ocean"

Company's come. In a ramshackle mansion, meet a family in the same condition—ancient, decayed. There's the brooding Duke, and his riotous brother. There's Grandam, lost in wilds of herself. There's a vicar, a philosopher, an angel, a ghost or two. And somewhere above them all, in a ruined garret…

"By turns delightfully black, singingly lyrical and/or innocently nonsensical. Here is a poet outside the mainstream with his own refreshingly original voice and bone[s] to pick." – Gillian Harding-Russell

PLUM STUFF by Rolli (Charles Anderson)
With illustrations by the author. Colour. 5.5 x 8.5. 128 pages. $18.88

Literate. Illiterate. Bewitching…. In his debut collection—a nine part whimsical discourse—Canadian author/artist Rolli waxes poetic about everything under "the muscular sun." There are poems about peaches and plums, about desperate celebs and monster poets, mistresses and mummified cats. Strange, celebratory, self-mocking, these are poems to be gulped down like summer fruit.

Rollick with Rolli through coddled lawns and parlour rooms, sloshing tea with gingercats under bluebird moons and slopping wine with bathing bachelorette hieresses in a world plum-stuffed with all things epicurean and bewitching, from English to Egyptian, the pathologic and the philosophic. By Canada's Charles Anderson (Rolli), recipient of the 2007 John Kenneth Galbraith Literary Award; and winner of the 2008 Commonwealth Short Story Competition.

KOLKATA DREAMS by K. Gandhar Chakravarty
88 pages, Colour, Illustrated. 5.5 x 8.5. ISBN 978-0-9809108-7-2. $18.88

Kolkata Dreams is a work of travel poetry that will transport you across the sea to northeastern India. The poems explore the idealization of Mother India against the realities of its westernization from the perspective of a Canadian-born Indo-North American discovering his heritage for the first time. When reading and reciting this poetry (you may be forced to voice these poems aloud), you will find that laughter often chokes itself on tears while the book yo-yos between meditation and contemplation. The experimental use of a first-person/third-person singular-detached narrator encapsulates the feeling of disembodiment often felt by the voyager, especially in this case, as the poet simultaneously belongs to yet remains apart from the cultures he explores. In short, Kolkata Dreams is a must-read for anyone interested in the balance between tradition and modernity, particularly in the context of globalization and twenty-first century India.

HYPODROME - Selected Poems by Jason Price Everett
148 pages. ISBN 978-1-926716-12-1 $18.88

"Begin anywhere. Stop anywhere. Everything that can possibly be written now is a drop of rain upon its vast syncretic ocean... This future of our shared media Byzantium is obscenely bright."

Jason Price Everett's poetry explodes from the page with the raucous power of industrial machinery and strikes its targets with the rapier's fine point. Honing in on the chaos of the past two decades, Hypodrome charts the growth of today's artist searching for the defining aesthetic of our time. These poems document the plastic, the losses, the frustrations and the triumphs accumulated during the course of an accelerated era, set against the backdrop of an ominously beautiful future.

MAPLE VEDAS by K. Gandhar Chakravarty
Colour with Original Artwork | 6 x 9 | 78 pages | ISBN 978-1-926716-05-3 | $18.88

The latest in a long line of scriptures, MAPLE VEDAS explores the voyages of the Gods of India – Vishnu, Shiva, Ganesha, Kali – as they visit the northwestern lands of the globe in the past, the present, and the near future. Peopled with other characters like a prophetic moose, a secretive walrus, and a charming groundhog, the interactions and dialogues of this third millenium testament force you to rethink history, religion, and your place in all of it – wherever you come from. In Maple Vedas, we discover that the Gods of India continue to roam Canada and the United States – perhaps standing beside you on a city bus – but they have come in new incarnations. Will you recognize them?

A DIRT ROAD HANGS FROM THE SKY by Claudia Serea
5 x 8. 130 pages, ISBN 978-1-926716-24-4 . $14.88

Beautiful, moving and brave; Claudia Serea's poems tell a story of fear and repression, but also one of hope. This strong collection speaks out against systems of repression all over the world, with a message that is vital and a powerful voice.

Written in unsparing, haunting detail, Claudia Serea's unforgettable A Dirt Road Hangs From the Sky brings to life the horrors of the brutal Communist repression in her native Romania in the second part of the 20th century – the prisons, the torture, the barbarous inhumanity – preserving in memory a time that should never be forgotten. She writes: "Tell me, grandma, everything you know / so I can be your mouth when you are gone." The grief is lasting; memory must serve as justice.

– Charles Rammelkamp, editor of *The Potomac Review,* author of *Fusen Bakudan*

NOT FOR ART NOR PRAYER by Darren C. Demaree
5. 5 x 8.5 | 90 pages | ISBN 978-1-926716-35-0 (pbk.) | $15.88

"...these poems gallop & salivate, these poems roar through their quiet deftness on the page. Congratulations for picking up this book, you're in for quite a ride." —Sam Sax, author of "sad boy / detective"

"...artful and prayerful..." "...these generously attentive and marvelously whimsical poems repeatedly resist sleight-of-hand poetic transubstantiation, while slyly acknowledging the inevitably transformative nature of language." —Lee Ann Roripaugh, Author of Dandarians

AS WE REFER TO OUR BODIES by Darren C. Demaree
5 x 8 . 90 pages. ISBN 978-1-926716-16-9 $15.88

Our bodies, our individual and collective bodies, and the separate bodies that together combine to make our systems, ecological, biological, psychological and technological— these are the bodies that we refer to, these are the bodies that Darren C. Demaree has dance for us on the page; nuanced or naked, dissected, desecrated and decorated; these are the bodies that rise and swell to the touch of the poet's pen.

"...a dangerous dreamer..." "unsettling in necessary ways."— Christopher Michel, Author, Editor